Sharing the Word

Against Protestant Popes

An Exegetical Study of
1 Peter 5:1-4

By:

Clay A. Kahler

Wipf & Stock
PUBLISHERS
Eugene, Oregon

Wipf and Stock Publishers
199 W 8th Ave, Suite 3
Eugene, OR 97401

Against Protestant Popes
An Exegetical Study of 1 Peter 5:1-4
By Kahler, Clay A.
Copyright©2005 by Kahler, Clay A.
ISBN: 1-59752-149-3
Publication date 4/19/2005

Special thanks to those who helped make this work possible:

Dr. George Goolde

Dr. Gary Coombs

Prof. Thomas Rohm

Dr. George Hare

Dr. Garland Shin

Dr. Tony Crisp

Prof. David Myers

The staff and faculty at Southern California Bible College & Seminary

The Members of First Baptist Church of Orrick Missouri

Table of Contents

Foreword

I have read everything that pastor Kahler has written. And I am not just referring to his published works. I have read virtually all of his undergraduate and seminary papers, including thesis and doctrinal summary, his magazine articles, the whole shooting match, so to speak. And while I am not without personal bias, Clay is my best friend, after all, I can honestly say that *Against Protestant Popes* is the best he has yet produced.

I say yet produced, because Clay is relatively young, and, if the Lord allows, I expect even greater works to come. But *Against Protestant Popes* is intelligent, informative, witty, and even useful. By useful, I mean that this work is more than a series of scholarly observations. In our world of inflated egos, and power crazed aspirations, *Against Protestant Popes* points out exactly how a pastor or elder is expected to behave. And not just from a personal opinion, but from a scriptural perspective. What Pastor Kahler has done is help define exactly what power a spiritual leader should exert, and maybe more importantly, what he shouldn't!

I have known Clay for quite a few years. He has been my student. Which is to say, that I have had him in some of my classes at Southern California Bible College and Seminary. He has been a fellow student. By which I mean that we have both taken classes together. He has been my boss. I have served as both his assistant pastor, and later, as his associate. And he is my friend, and brother in Christ. As I said at the beginning of this forward, I am not without personal bias. That being said, I believe that this book will help the reader to understand better the relationship between the pastor, the elders, and the congregation. And those relationships are of such importance in our Christian society, that they can make or break the walk of a new convert, or even torpedo the walk of a mature believer! And so I recommend whole-heartedly this work, and eagerly await pastor Kahler's next book, whatever and whenever that may come!

Dr. David Myers
Senior Pastor, Ridgewood Baptist Church
Bemidji, Minnesota

Introduction

(1 Peter 5:1-4)

Πρεσβυτέρους τούς ἐν ὑμῖν παρακαλῶ ὁ συμπρεσβύτερος καὶ μάρτυς τῶν τοῦ Χριστοῦ παθημάτων, ὁ καὶ τῆς μελλούσης ἀποκαλύπτεσθαι δόξης κοινωνός· ποιμάνατε τὸ ἐν ὑμῖν ποίμνιον τοῦ θεοῦ ἐπισκοποῦντες μὴ ἀναγκαστῶς ἀλλ ἑκουσίως, μηδὲ αἰσχροκερδῶς ἀλλὰ προθύμως, μηδὲ ὡς κατακυριεύοντες τῶν κλήρων ἀλλὰ τύποι γινόμενοι τοῦ ποιμνίου· καὶ φανερωθέντος τοῦ ἀρχιποίμενος κομιεῖσθε τὸν ἀμαράντινον τῆς δόξης στέφανον.

The elders who are among you I encourage as a fellow elder and witness of the sufferings of Christ the partner of the glory about to be revealed, shepherd the flock of God among you see to not under compulsion but willingly nor with greediness for material gain but eagerly, nor as having power over the share but as a pattern to the flock. And at the appearing of the Chief Shepherd, you will receive the unfading crown of glory.

The overall theme of the book of First Peter seems to be "Suffering and security produce joy." It is with this in mind that we must look at Chapter 5 verses 1-4. Peter speaks in the previous chapters to the valor of suffering, the patience produced through suffering and the lessons learned through suffering[1].

Probably written near A.D. 64, Peter would have been aware of the persecutions that, though scattered were on going. He would have no doubt realized that they were to increase. In fact the letter is addressed to "the pilgrims of the Dispersion in Pontus, Galatia, Cappadocia, Asia, and Bithynia." The dispersion in itself was a result of previous persecution.

Though chapter 5:1-4 may seem to be detached from the overall theme of the book, I believe that it is integrally connected. It is in the midst of suffering that the flock would most need elders who are willingly and eagerly shepherding the flock. It is in the midst of persecution that they will need leaders who do not "rule over" them but lead from among them.

Christian leaders are servants, not masters. This New Testament theme is reaffirmed here, with a word about leaders' motives. Leaders must want to serve; indeed, they must be willing, and even "eager to serve." People have many different motives for wanting to be leaders. But a passionate desire to serve others is a basic qualification for Christian leadership.

---

[1] We must keep in mind that Peter is an "authority" in this matter. It was he, and the other apostles who rejoiced after having been beaten for the sake of the gospel, because they were "counted worthy to suffer shame for His [Christ] name" (Acts 5:41).

Chapter 1

(1 Peter 5:1-4: Verse-by-Verse Translation and Commentary)

The ultimate purpose of exegesis is to gain a fuller and clearer understanding of a given text. It is with this goal in mind that we will begin our commentary of each verse with a "key word analysis."

Another reason for this method is our shared belief of the *plenary verbal inspiration* of the Scriptures. If we believe (and we do) that every single word is the result of the inspiration of the Holy Spirit it becomes imperative to become intimately familiar with each word.

Using a variety of sources along with my own word studies, we will look at the common meaning of each word. This will enable us to better translate and comment on each verse. With this in mind let us begin this process with verse one.

Verse 1
Πρεσβυτέρους τοὺς ἐν ὑμῖν παρακαλῶ ὁ συμπρεσβύτερος καὶ μάρτυς τῶν τοῦ Χριστοῦ παθημάτων, ὁ καὶ τῆς μελλούσης ἀποκαλύπτεσθαι δόξης κοινωνός·
The elders who are among you I encourage as a fellow elder and witness of the sufferings of Christ the partner of the glory about to be revealed,

Key Word Analysis	
Πρεσβυτέρους	*Adjective Accusative Masculine Plural* **Meaning and Occurrence.** 1. *presbýteros*, comparative of *présbys*, means a. "older," or simply "old," with no negative connotations but rather a sense of venerability. It then comes into use b. for presidents, members of various guilds, committees etc., village officials, executive committees of priests, and senior groups of different types. c. In the Jewish and Christian sphere it is often hard to distinguish between the designation of age and the title of office. Age is clearly the point in Gen. 18:11-12 and Jn. 8:9; Acts 2:17. Elsewhere the *presbýteroi* are the bearers of a tradition (Mt. 15:2), and a title is at issue when the reference is to members of governing bodies, as in the nation, the synagogue, or the church. 2. *tó presbytérion*, which occurs in pre-Christian works only in Sus. 50 for the "dignity of elders," occurs in the NT for a. "the Sanhedrin," and b. "the council of elders" in the church (cf. Lk. 22:66; 1 Tim. 4:14). Common in Ignatius, the term signifies for him the council of presbyters, which parallels that of the

	apostles (*Philadelphians* 5.1) and functions as the bishop's council (8.1). 3. The *sympresbýteros* is the "fellow elder" (1 Pet. 5:5); it becomes a common collegial form used by bishops in addressing presbyters.[2]
παρακαλῶ	*Verb Indicative Present Active First Person Singular* **Thayer Definition:** 1) to call to one's side, call for, summon 2) to address, speak to, (call to, call upon), which may be done in the way of exhortation, entreaty, comfort, instruction, etc. 2a) to admonish, exhort 2b) to beg, entreat, beseech 2b1) to strive to appease by entreaty 2c) to console, to encourage and strengthen by consolation, to comfort 2c1) to receive consolation, be comforted 2d) to encourage, strengthen 2e) exhorting and comforting and encouraging 2f) to instruct, teach[3]
ὁ συμπρεσβύτερος	*Noun Nominative Masculine Singular* A compound word meaning (συν) together and (πρεσβυτερους) elder. Translated fellow elder it carries the

---

[2]Kittel, Gerhard, and Friedrich, Gerhard, Editors, *The Theological Dictionary of the New Testament,* Grand Rapids, Michigan: William B. Eerdmans Publishing Company 1985.
[3] Thayers Greek Definitions

	connotation of equality in service.
μάρτυς	*Noun Nominative Masculine Singular* a *witness* (literally [judicially] or figuratively [generally]); by analogy a "martyr":—martyr, record, witness.[4]
Χριστοῦ	*Noun Genitive Masculine Singular* Peter was indeed a witness of the sufferings of Christ when on his trial, and doubtless also when he was scourged and mocked, and when he was crucified. After his denial of his Lord, he wept bitterly, and evidently then followed him to The place where he was crucified, and, in company with others, observed with painful solicitude the last agonies of his Savior.[5]
παθημάτων	*Noun Genitive Neuter Plural* From a presumed derivative of G3806 (πάθος); something *undergone*, that is, *hardship* or *pain*; subjectively an *emotion* or *influence:*—affection, affliction, motion, suffering.[6]
μελλούσης	*Verb Participle Present Active Genitive Feminine Singular* μέλλω (before an infinitive) *be going, be about, intend; must, be destined;* (participle without infinitive) *coming, future;* (finite verb without infinitive) *delay, wait* (τί μέλλεις *what are you waiting for? Ac 22:16*).
ἀποκαλύπτεσθαι	*Verb Infinitive Present Passive* Peter also referred to himself as **one**

[4] Strong, James, *Strongs Hebrew and Greek Dictionaries*
[5] Barnes, Albert, *Barnes Notes on the New Testament*
[6] Strong, James, *Strongs Hebrew and Greek Dictionaries*

	who... will share (κοινονος; 1 Peter 4:13) **in the glory to be revealed.** Peter had just made the point that those who share in Christ's sufferings will also share in His glory (4:13).
δόξης	*Noun Genitive Feminine Singular* *glory* (as very *apparent*), in a wide application (literally or figuratively, objectively or subjectively):—dignity, glory (-ious), honour, praise, worship[7]
κοινωνός	*Noun Nominative Masculine Singular* **Thayer Definition:** 1) a partner, associate, comrade, companion 2) a partner, sharer, in anything [8]

Peter is addressing the elders (Πρεσβυτέρους) among "the elect who are sojourners of the Dispersion in Pontus, Galatia, Cappadocia, Asia, and Bithynia" (1 Peter 1:1). It is important to notice the position of these elders, "among" the flock (ἐν ὑμῖν). He begins by encouraging them in the proper manner of shepherding the Flock of God, which is entrusted, to them (v.2-3). Peter makes an interesting assertion here. He encourages the elders, not as an Apostle, not as one of the three chosen by Christ as His "inner-circle," "but as a fellow elder." A.T. Robertson has an interesting article about this association by Peter with his recipients:

> "Who am a fellow-elder (ὁ συμπρεσβύτερος). Earliest use of this compound in an inscription of B.C. 120 for fellow-elders (alderman) in a town, here only in N.T., in eccles. writers. For the word Πρεσβυτέρους in the technical sense

---

[7] Strong, James, *Strongs Hebrew and Greek Dictionaries*
[8] Thayers Greek Definitions

of officers in a Christian church (like elder in the local synagogues of the Jews) see Acts 11:30; 20:17. It is noteworthy that here Peter the Apostle (1:1) calls himself an elder along with (συν) the other 'elders.[9]'"

He then identifies himself as "witness of the sufferings of Christ the partner of the glory about to be revealed."

1. **"A witness of the sufferings of Christ"**- Peter identified himself as a witness (μαρτυς) just as Jesus had said they would be (Acts 1:8) and what Peter claimed to be (Acts 3:15; 10:39).

2. **"A partner of the glory about to be revealed."**- Peter had no misconception about the doctrine of eternal security. We can see the theme of our partaking in the Glory to come here: Luke 5:10; 2 Cor 1:7; 2 Peter 1:4. See same idea in Rom 8:17-18

---

[9] Robertson, A.T., *Word Pictures of the New Testament,* "1 Peter"

Verse 2	
ποιμάνατε τὸ ἐν ὑμῖν ποίμνιον τοῦ θεοῦ ἐπισκοποῦντες μὴ ἀναγκαστῶς ἀλλ ἑκουσίως, μηδὲ αἰσχροκερδῶς ἀλλὰ προθύμως,	
shepherd the flock of God among you see to not under compulsion but willingly nor with greediness for material gain but eagerly, ·	

Key Word Analysis	
ποιμάνατε	*Verb Imperative Aorist Active Second Person Plural* tend like a shepherd; rule; keep sheep (Lk 17:7); π. ἑαυτόν care only for oneself (Jude 1:12)
ποίμνιον	*Noun Accusative Neuter Singular* 1) a flock (especially) of sheep 2) a group of Christ's disciples 3) bodies of Christian (churches) presided over by elders[10]
τοῦ θεοῦ	*Noun Genitive Masculine Singular* masculine *God* (κατα θεόν *according to God's will, godly; after the likeness of God* Eph 4:24); *god;* feminine *goddess* (Ac 19:37)
ἐπισκοποῦντες	*Verb Participle Present Active Nominative Masculine Second Person Plural* See to it, take care; oversee, see after
ἀναγκαστῶς	*Adverb* under compulsion; duress; obligation
ἑκουσίως	*Adverb* Willingly; deliberately- This word has more than a simple willingness indicated, it also includes a level of deliberation to it. We must be willing in our service but we must

---

[10] Thayers Greek Definitions

	also serve with a purpose.
αἰσχροκερδῶς	*Adverb* with greediness for material gain- A.T. Roberts said, "A compound adverb not found elsewhere, but the old adjective *aischrokerdēs* is in 1 Tim 3:8; Titus 1:7. See also Titus 1:11 "for the sake of filthy lucre" (*aischrou kerdous charin*). Clearly the elders received stipends, else there could be no such temptation.[11]
προθύμως	*Adverb* willingly, with alacrity, eagerness, enthusiasm, zeal

The image of a "shepherd" is that of a concerned guide, not of a severe ruler (although the image of shepherds had been applied to rulers in parts of the ancient Near East). Charges of illegitimate gain were often made against moral teachers in the ancient world, and it was necessary for Christians to avoid even the appearance of impropriety. (Like certain officials in the Jewish community, these Christian leaders distributed the funds for the poor.)[12]

Peter said that he was encouraging the elders to correctly minister to the "flock of God among them. Just how is that? First do not do so "under compulsion." Do not attempt to minister to God's people out of a sense of obligation. This could mean obligation to the flock or even obligation to God. Ministering as a servant of God to His flock is a privilege that is entrusted to us. We should not feel as though we are under duress. In fact Peter then says that we are to minister willingly. Peter uses the word ἀναγκαστῶς to get his point a crossed. Thayer Definitions says, by force or constrain.

---

[11] Robertson, Archibald Thomas, *Word Pictures in the New Testament, Vol. 6: General Epistles & Revelation*
[12] Keener, Craig S., *IVP Bible Background Commentary: New Testament (1Peter)*, Wheaton Il: IVP Press

He then looks at the "flip-side" of the coin. There are those whose entire ministry is driven by the amount of money that they can accumulate. There are Christian ministers who will not speak for less than twenty five thousand dollars per engagement[13]. Peter, no doubt, remembered the message of Christ to the disciples, that we are not to worry about from where our needs would be met (Matt 6:25-33). Do not be an elder for the sake of financial gain (1 Tim 3:3, Titus 1:11), but humbly and willingly, eagerly, knowing that God will supply all of your needs. It is apparent that the elders received some form of wage for their services, otherwise this would not be a temptation.

---

[13] www.ChristianSpeakers.com

Verse 3
μηδὲ ὡς κατακυριεύοντες τῶν κλήρων ἀλλὰ τύποι γινόμενοι τοῦ ποιμνίου·
nor as having power over the share but as a pattern to the flock.

Key Word Analysis	
κατακυριεύοντες	*Verb Participle Present Active Nominative Masculine Second Person Plural* This compound word is made up of Κατα, meaning "over," in respect to authority (according to *Nestle Aland Dictionary* p.93)[14]. And Κυριευω, which has the understanding of "jurisdiction over." Therefore it is often rendered "overseeing" or "having power over." Notice the constant theme of the word below, ruling from above. It carries with it the concept of detached, aloof rule. It also seems to include the concept of seizure of authority.
τῶν κλήρων	*Noun Genitive Masculine Plural* what is obtained by lot, allotted portion; a portion of the ministry common to the apostles; used of the part which one will have in eternal salvation; of salvation itself: the eternal salvation which God has assigned to the saints: of persons[15]
τύποι	*Noun Nominative Masculine Plural* pattern, example, model, standard (γράψας ἐπιστολὴν ἔχουσαν τὸν ττοῦτον he wrote a letter that went like this Ac 3:25); type, figure (of someone to

[14] This differs from the normative meaning of κατα. This word normally appears in two forms. When in the Genitive, it is usually translated down, upon, against. However when seen in the Accusative case, it is rendered long, according to. Though this is the norm, it is not out of the scope of the word to, in the context of authority, to translate κατα as over. Notice the consistent theme of position of rule, "**overpower**," "show one's authority **over**," "to gain dominion **over**," "to exercise dominion **over**," "lord **over**," etc.

[15] *Thayers Greek Definitions*

	come in the future Rom 5:14); scar, mark (Jn 20:25); image, statue (Ac 7:43); warning (1 Cor 10:6)
γινόμενοι	*Verb Participle Present Middle or Passive Deponent Nominative Masculine Second Person Plural* become, be; happen, take place, arise (aorist often impersonal it happened or came about); come into being, be born or created; be done (of things) become something (of persons); come, go (γ. κατά arrive off Ac 27:7); appear (Mk 1:4; Jn 1:6); marry (Rom 7:3, 4); μή γένοιτο no indeed!; sometimes with dative of person have, possess, receive (for example Mt 18:12)
τοῦ ποιμνίου	*Noun Genitive Neuter Singular* 1) a flock (especially) of sheep 2) a group of Christ's disciples 3) bodies of Christian (churches) presided over by elders[16]

Peter is now moving in a new direction. Before he admonished the elders to refrain from greed and compulsion. But here he uses much stronger language. The New King James version reads like this, *"nor as being lords over those entrusted to you."* Peter is dealing with an issue of "trust." He suggests that acting like a tyrant is some sort of breech of that trust. Additionally, Peter's use of the participial κατακυριεύοντες, is remarkable (See word study Chapter 4).

This verse deals with more than overpowering tyranny; it ends with then admonition, "but being examples to the flock." Wuest put is this way:

---

[16] Thayers Greek Definitions

"The word translated 'ensample' means 'a print left as an impression after a blow has been struck, a pattern or a model of something else.' Under-shepherds should be living patterns or models of the Chief Shepherd, the Lord Jesus.[17]"

So many pastors are so busy being separated from their flock that they cannot be examples. We must be known by the people before they can see us model Christ.

---

[17] Wuest, Kenneth S., *Wuest's Word Studies From the Greek New Testament Vol Two*, Grand Rapids: Eerdmans Publishing, 1942. (p125)

Verse 4
καὶ φανερωθέντος τοῦ ἀρχιποίμενος κομιεῖσθε τὸν ἀμαράντινον τῆς δόξης στέφανον.
And at the appearing of the Chief Shepherd, you will receive the unfading crown of glory.

Key Word Analysis	
φανερωθέντος	*Verb Participle Aorist Passive Genitive Masculine Singular* make known, reveal, show; make evident or plain; passive be revealed or made known; be evident or plain; appear, reveal oneself
τοῦ ἀρχιποίμενος	*Noun Genitive Masculine Singular* Chief Shepherd- The prince of the pastors—the Lord Jesus Christ. "Peter, in the passage above, ranks himself with the elders; here he ranks Christ himself with the pastors"—Benson.[18]
κομιεῖσθε	*Verb Indicative Future Middle Second Person Plural* to receive, obtain: the promised blessing; to receive what was previously one's own, to get back, receive back, recover
τὸν ἀμαράντινον	*Adjective Accusative Masculine Singular* From G263; "amaranthine", that is, (by implication) fadeless: that fades not away.
τῆς δόξης	*Noun Genitive Feminine Singular* glory, splendor, grandeur (in genitive case often glorious); power, kingdom; praise, honor; pride (δόξα καὶ χαρά pride and joy 1 Th 2:20); brightness, brilliance; revealed presence of God, God himself; heaven (1 Ti 3:16); glorious heavenly being (2 Pe 2:10; Jude 1:8); δὸς δόξαν τῷ θεῷ promise before God to tell the truth (Jn 9:24)

---

[18] Barnes, Albert, *Barnes Notes on the New Testament*

στέφανον	*Noun Accusative Masculine Singular* wreath, crown; prize, reward, gift; reason for pride or boasting (Php 4:1; 1 Th 2:19)

Peter, always looking for the return of His Lord, makes this statement. Look at the certainty that Peter exudes as he speaks of Christ's return. It is interesting to note also, Peter's relating Jesus to the elder. He says that the elder is to be a shepherd to the flock, as Christ is the Chief Shepherd.

ἀρχιποίμενος is a compound word.

ἀρχή- *chief* (in various applications of order, time, place or rank):—beginning, corner, (at the, the) first (estate), magistrate, power, principality, principle, rule.

Ποιμήν- Of uncertain affinity; a *shepherd* (literally or figuratively):—shepherd, pastor.

It is interesting that this word could be translated "The Ruling Shepherd." That should cause any man of God to pause before he declares that he is in charge. Jesus Himself used similar terminology in John 10: 11-14 when He said,

> "I am the **good shepherd**. The good shepherd gives His life for the sheep. But a hireling, he who is not the shepherd, one who does not own the sheep, sees the wolf coming and leaves the sheep and flees; and the wolf catches the sheep and scatters them. The hireling flees because he is a hireling and does not care about the sheep. I am the **good shepherd**; and I know My sheep, and am known by My own.

We must be careful not to, in our arrogance, try to play the role of the Chief Shepherd. Christ has entrusted elders with a great and awesome task. That is to equip the saints, guide and nourish them. That in itself should be enough. But we are promised even more.

"...you will receive the unfading crown of glory" At the coming of Christ,[19] elders are promised to receive a reward, an unfading crown (στέφανον) of Glory.

Unfading (ἀμαράντινον)

- Thayer Definition: composed of amaranth; a flower so called because it never withers or fades, and when plucked off revives if moistened with water; a symbol of perpetuity and immortality

- It might be compared to the Christian's glorious inheritance (1 Pet 1:3-5) that is pure, undefiled, unstained (ἀμίαντον), and unfading or permanent (ἀμάραντον).

Crown (στέφανον)

- In the Gospels it is used only of the crown of thorns, but Jesus is crowned with glory and honor (Heb 2:9). In all these passages it is the crown of victory as it is here.

- *Stephanos* means a chaplet (wreath) made of leaves or leaf-like gold, used for marriage and festive occasions, and expressing public recognition of victory in races, games and war; also **figuratively** as a reward for efficient Christian life and service. This symbol was more noticeable and intricate than the plain fillet. Only in the Rev of John is στεφανος, στεφανος, *stephanos* called "golden." The "crown of thorns" which Jesus wore was a *stephanos* (woven wreath) of thorns; the kind is not known (Mt 27:29; Mk 15:17; Jn 19:2,5)[20].

---

[19] Presumably this applies to the elders who endeavor to shepherd the flock without compulsion, even willingly and without regard to financial gain, and who do not make it a habit of lording over the flock.

[20] Orr, James. International Standard Bible Encyclopedia Vol II, Grand Rapids: Eerdmans, 1939. p762

Of glory (τῆς δόξης)

- Translated, "of Glory," this word speaks of the reward itself. It is not a comment on the composition of the crown but the circumstance under which it will be awarded.
- Much like an athlete would receive the victory crown (στέφανος), so shall the elder.

Chapter 2

(Diagramming)

In his book, Principals and Practice of Greek Exegesis, Dr. John D. Grassmick said, "Diagramming is a grammatical visual aid. When the exegete has the words of the text laid out visually before him, he is able to wrestle with their meaning with greater ease and proficiency. It is a means to this greater end!"

It is with this goal in mind that we look that the word relationships in this graphic method. This section is separated into two sections.

Section one is a grammatical analysis designed to primarily identify parts of speech and thus identify their function in the context of the passage.

Section is the actual diagram. It is, as Dr. Grassmick said, a visual tool to demonstrate the grammatical relationships of each word within the passage. It is designed to allow us to evaluate the meaning of this passage at the deepest level and thus allow us to better explore its depths.

Πρεσβυτέρους²¹ οὖν ἐν ὑμῖν²² παρακαλῶ²³ ὁ συμπρεσβύτερος²⁴ καὶ μάρτυς²⁵ τῶν τοῦ Χριστοῦ²⁶ παθημάτων²⁷, ὁ καὶ τῆς μελλούσης²⁸ ἀποκαλύπτεσθαι²⁹ δόξης³⁰ κοινωνός·³¹ ποιμάνατε³² τὸ ἐν ὑμῖν³³ ποίμνιον³⁴ τοῦ θεοῦ³⁵ ἐπισκοποῦντες³⁶ μὴ ἀναγκαστῶς³⁷ ἀλλ ἑκουσίως³⁸, μηδὲ αἰσχροκερδῶς³⁹ ἀλλὰ προθύμως⁴⁰, μηδὲ ὡς κατακυριεύοντες⁴¹ τῶν κλήρων⁴² ἀλλὰ τύποι⁴³ γινόμενοι⁴⁴ τοῦ ποιμνίου·⁴⁵ καὶ φανερωθέντος⁴⁶ τοῦ ἀρχιποίμενος⁴⁷ κομιεῖσθε⁴⁸ τὸν ἀμαράντινον⁴⁹ τῆς δόξης⁵⁰ στέφανον⁵¹.

---

[21] Masculine Plural Accusative (Direct Object)
[22] Second Person Plural Locative (Place)
[23] Present Active Indicative First Person Singular
[24] Masculine Singular Nominative (Subject)
[25] Masculine Singular Nominative (Subject)
[26] Masculine Singular Genitive (Possession)
[27] Neuter Plural Genitive (Reference)
[28] Present Active Participle Feminine Singular Genitive (Time)
[29] Present Passive Infinitive
[30] Feminine Singular Genitive (Descriptive)
[31] Masculine Singular Nominative (Subject)
[32] Aorist Active Imperative Second Person Plural
[33] Second Person Plural Locative (Place)
[34] Neuter Singular Accusative (Direct Object)
[35] Masculine Singular Genitive (Possessive)
[36] Present Active Participle Masculine Second Person Plural Nominative
[37] Adverb
[38] Adverb
[39] Adverb
[40] Adverb
[41] Present Active Participle Masculine Second Person Plural Nominative (Subject)
[42] Masculine Plural Genitive (Direct Object)
[43] Masculine Plural Nominative (Subject)
[44] Present Passive Deponent Participle Masculine Second Person Plural Nominative
[45] Neuter Singular Genitive (Reference)
[46] Aorist Passive Participle Masculine Singular Genitive (Time)
[47] Masculine Singular Genitive (Description)
[48] Future Middle Indicative Second Person Plural
[49] Masculine Singular Accusative (Simple Apposition)
[50] Feminine Singular Genitive (Material)
[51] Masculine Singular Accusative (Direct Object)

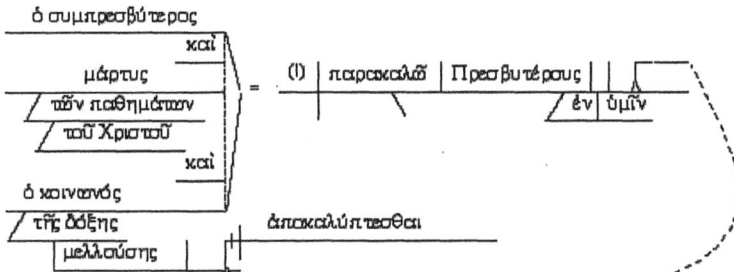

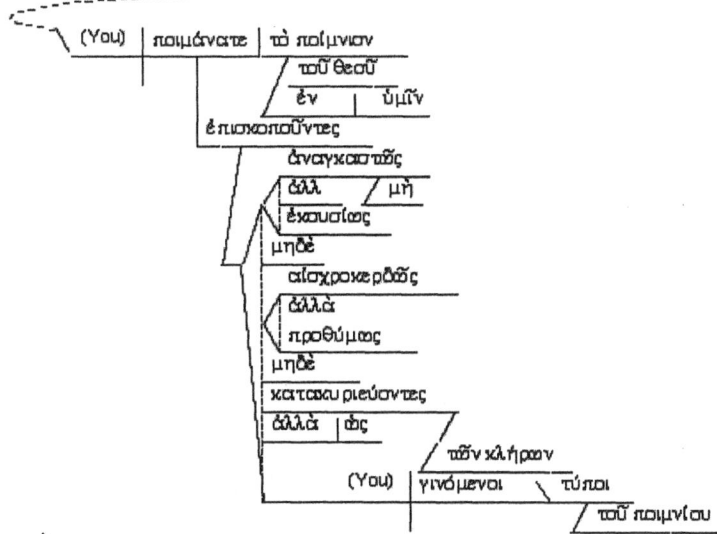

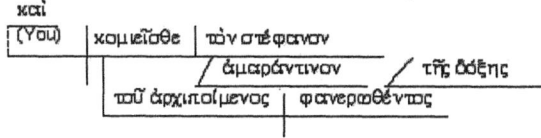

Chapter 3

(Grammatical Analysis)

Grammatical analysis represents considerations at a number of levels. The first and most basic is the morphological, which information is found within the word itself. This includes information, which is distinctive for a given form when viewed from the whole of a paradigm. For example, Θηεος is distinctively nominative in case, masculine in gender, and singular in number. This morphological information is usually straightforward and noncontroversial.

Πρεσβυτέρους	Masculine Plural Accusative (Direct Object)
ἐν	Preposition Locative (Sphere)
ὑμῖν	Second Person Plural Locative (Sphere) *(ἐν ὑμῖν)This is significant because it relates the position of the elders that Peter is addressing. He is not speaking to some hierarchy but to the elders who are among the people.*
παρακαλῶ	Present Active Indicative First Person Singular
ὁ συμπρεσβύτερος	Masculine Singular Nominative

	(Subject) *Peter could have addressed himself in any number of ways, Apostle, One of the Twelve, Senior Elder, but he chose to align himself with those to whom he was writing.*
καὶ	Coordinate Conjunction
μάρτυς	Masculine Singular Nominative (Subject) *The reader will notice that there are three separate nouns identified as the subject. Here is a compound subject each referring to Peter.*
τοῦ Χριστοῦ	Masculine Singular Genitive (Reference)
τῶν	Article Neuter Plural Genitive (Reference)
παθημάτων	Neuter Plural Genitive (Reference)
ὁ	Article Masculine Singular Nominative
καὶ	Coordinate Conjunction
τῆς	Article Present Active Participle Feminine Singular Genitive (Time)
μελλούσης	Present Active Participle Feminine Singular Genitive (Time)
ἀποκαλύπτεσθαι	Present Passive Infinitive
δόξης	Feminine Singular Genitive (Descriptive)
κοινωνός	Masculine Singular Nominative (Subject)
ποιμάνατε	Aorist Active Imperative Second Person Plural *Notice that this an imperative or a command. Elders are commanded to shepherd the flock according to the principles to follow.*

τὸ	Article Accusative Neuter Singular
ἐν	Preposition Locative (Sphere)
ὑμῖν	Second Person Plural Locative (Sphere) *Peter, again, uses the prepositional phrase, (ἐν ὑμῖν). This could be for emphasis, stressing the necessity of shepherding from among or within the flock.*
ποίμνιον	Accusative Neuter Singular
τοῦ	Article Masculine Singular Genitive (Possessive)
θεοῦ	Masculine Singular Genitive (Possessive) *(τοῦ θεοῦ) We must never forget whose flock it is that we have been trusted to lead.*
ἐπισκοποῦντες	Present Active Participle Masculine Second Person Plural Nominative (Means)
μὴ	Negative Particle
ἀναγκαστῶς	Adverb
ἀλλ	Subordinating Conjunction
ἑκουσίως	Adverb
μηδὲ	Coordinating Conjunction
αἰσχροκερδῶς	Adverb
ἀλλὰ	Subordinating Conjunction
προθύμως	Adverb
μηδὲ	Coordinating Conjunction
ὡς	Subordinating Conjunction
κατακυριεύοντες	Present Active Participle Masculine Second Person Plural Nominative (Subject)

τῶν	Article Masculine Plural Genitive (Subordinating)
κλήρων	Masculine Plural Genitive (Subordinating)
ἀλλὰ	Subordinating Conjunction
τύποι	Masculine Plural Nominative (Subject)
γινόμενοι	Present Passive Deponent Participle Masculine Second Person Plural Nominative (Subject) *Though often translated as becoming, here it is clear that they are to be rather than become examples to those in their care.*
τοῦ	Article Neuter Singular Genitive (Reference)
ποιμνίου	Neuter Singular Genitive (Reference)
Καὶ	Coordinating Conjunction
φανερωθέντος	Aorist Passive Participle Masculine Singular Genitive (Genitive Absolute)
τοῦ	Article Masculine Singular Genitive (Genitive Absolute)
ἀρχιποίμενος	Masculine Singular Genitive (Genitive Absolute)
κομιεῖσθε	Future Middle Indicative Second Person Plural
τὸν	Article Adjective Masculine Singular Accusative
ἀμαράντινον	Adjective Masculine Singular Accusative
τῆς	Article Feminine Singular Genitive (Material)
δόξης	Feminine Singular Genitive (Material)
στέφανον	Masculine Singular Accusative (Direct Object)

Chapter 4
(Word Studies)

Καταχυριεύω (2634)
Κυριεύω (2961)

Being Lords Over

Καταχυριεύω

This compound word is made up of Κατα, meaning "over," in respect to authority (according to *Nestle Aland Dictionary* p.93)[52]. And Κυριευω, which has the understanding of "jurisdiction over." Therefore it is often rendered "overseeing" or "having power over." Notice the constant theme of the word below, ruling from above. It carries with it the concept of detached, aloof rule. It also seems to include the concept of seizure of authority.

---

[52] This differs from the normative meaning of κατα. This word normally appears in two forms. When in the Genitive, it is usually translated *down, upon, against*. However when seen in the Accusative case, it is rendered *along, according to*. Though this is the norm, it is not out of the scope of the word to, in the context of authority, translate κατα as over. Notice the consistent theme of position of rule, "**over**power," "show one's authority **over**," "to gain dominion **over**," "to exercise dominion **over**," "lord **over**," etc.

New Testament Definitions:

A CONCISE GREEK-ENGLISH DICTIONARY OF THE NEW TESTAMENT
   Κατακυριεύω-

have power over; overpower (Ac 19:16); try to show one's
authority over (1 Pe 5:3)

LIDDELL AND SCOTT'S GREEK-ENGLISH LEXICON
   Κατακυριεύω-

κατα-κυριεύω, to gain dominion over, c. gen., N.T.

NAS HEBREW AND GREEK DICTIONARIES
   Κατακυριεύω-

katakurieuō; from G2596 (κατά) and G2961(Κυριεύω);
to exercise dominion over:—lord it over (2), lording it over (1),
subdued (1).

   Κυριεύω-

kurieuō; from G2962 (Κύριος); *to be lord of, rule:*—has
jurisdiction over (1), Lord (1), lord it over (2), lords (1), master
over (2).

STRONG'S HEBREW AND GREEK DICTIONARIES
   Κατακυριεύω-

katakurieuō kat-ak-oo-ree-yoo'-o From G2596
(κατά) and G2961 (Κυριεύω); to lord against, that is, control,
subjugate:—exercise dominion over (lordship), be lord over,
overcome.

   Κυριεύω-

From G2962 (Κύριος); to *rule:*—have dominion over, lord, be
lord of, exercise lordship over.

THAYER DEFINITION
 Κατακυριεύω-

1) to bring under one's power, to subject one's self, to subdue, master
2) to hold in subjection, to be master of, exercise lordship over

Κυριεύω-
1) to be lord of, to rule, have dominion over
2) of things and forces
2a) to exercise influence upon, to have power over

ROBERTSON'S WORD PICTURES OF THE NEW TESTAMENT
 Κατακυριεύω-

Lording it over (*katakurieuontes*). Present active participle of *katakurieuō*, late compound (*kata, kurios*) as in Matt 20:25.

BARNES' NOTES ON THE NEW TESTAMENT
Neither as being lords—Margin, "overruling." The word here used (κατακυριεύω katakurieuō) is rendered "exercise dominion over," in Matt.20:25; exercise lordship over, in Mark 10:42; and overcame, in Acts 19:16. It does not elsewhere occur in the New Testament. It refers properly to that kind of jurisdiction which civil rulers or magistrates exercise. This is an exercise of authority, as contradistinguished from the influence of reason, persuasion, and example. The latter pertains to the ministers of religion; the former is forbidden to them. Their dominion is not to be that of temporal lordship; it is to be that of love and truth. This command would prohibit all assumption of temporal power by the ministers of religion, and all conferring of titles of nobility on those who are preachers of the gospel. It needs scarcely to be said that it has been very little regarded in the church.

New Testament Occurrences:

Κατακυριεύω (2634)

There are five occurrences of Κατακυριεύω in the New Testament.

1. **Matt 20:25-** But Jesus called them to Himself and said, "You know that the rulers of the Gentiles **lord it over them**, and those who are great exercise authority over them.
   Note: Here Jesus was speaking of the Gentile tyranny of the age.
2. **Mark 10:42-** But Jesus called them to Himself and said to them, "You know that those who are considered rulers over the Gentiles lord it over them, and their great ones **exercise authority** over them.
   Note: Here Jesus was speaking of the Gentile tyranny of the age.
3. **1 Pet 5:3-** nor as **being lords** over those entrusted to you, but being examples to the flock;
   Note: Here in our passage Peter is telling the elder that he is not to be like the descriptions of the Gentiles or the Pharisees in their leadership styles.
4. **Rev 17:14-** These will make war with the Lamb, and the Lamb will overcome them, for He is Lord of **lords** and King of kings; and those who are with Him are called, chosen, and faithful."
   Note: Notice the position of Christ as the Lord over those who are lording. This possibly demonstrates the unrighteousness of their rule.
5. **Acts 19:16-** Then the man in whom the evil spirit was leaped on them, **overpowered them**, and prevailed against them, so that they fled out of that house naked and wounded.
   Note: Here we see it in the context of demonic activity. It is a stretch to say that this word always carries with it the idea of demonic activity, however, it does carry the context of evil in each instance excepting Revelation 17:14.

Κατακυριεύω (2634)

This word carries with it a consistent idea of tyrannical authority. It is a word of conquest and oppression. This holds true even in Revelation 17:14, where Christ will conquer all who are rejecters of the Gospel of Christ.

Κυριεύω (2961)

There are eight occurrences of Κυριεύω in the New Testament.

1. **Rom 6:9-** knowing that Christ, having been raised from the dead, dies no more. Death no longer has **dominion** over Him.
    Note: No more having dominion, or control. Christ, as a result of His resurrection, is now outside of the grasp of the power of death.
2. **Rom 6:14-** For sin shall not have **dominion** over you, for you are not under law but under grace.

    Note: Again we see the concept of oppression.

3. **Rom 7:1-** Or do you not know, brethren (for I speak to those who know the law), that the law has **dominion** over a man as long as he lives?
    Note: The Law is seen here as a ruling authority over the life of one who is under it's control.
4. **2 Cor 1:24-** Not that we have **dominion** over your faith, but are fellow workers for your joy; for by faith you stand

    Note: Now we see the word used in context as one who would have power over the faith if another.
5. **Luke 22:25-** And He said to them, "The kings of the Gentiles **exercise lordship** over them, and those who exercise authority over them are called 'benefactors.'
    Note: Tyranny is the concept seen here.

6.   **Rom 14:9-** For to this end Christ died and rose and lived again, that He might be **Lord** of both the dead and the living.
     Note: Now seen in reference to the Lord, we see it in a positive light for the first time.

7.   **1 Tim 6:15-** which He will manifest in His own time, *He who is* the blessed and only Potentate, the King of kings and Lord of **lords,**
     Note: Again in reference to Christ's dominion this time over the lords of the earth.

8.   **Luke 22:25-** And He said to them, "The kings of the Gentiles **exercise lordship** over them, and those who exercise authority over them are called 'benefactors.'
     Note: Here we again see the tyranny of the Gentile authority.

Κυριεύω (2961)

This, the root word of Κατακυριεύω shares the same idea. Notice the trend above. Each time that the word is used to refer to man's rule it is negative or even evil in its concept. However, when referring to the Lord Jesus it demonstrates a righteous rule.

Old Testament Occurrences:

Κατακυριεύω (2634)

There are nine occurrences of Κατακυριεύω in the (Septuagint) Old Testament.

1.   **Nu 21:24-** Then Israel **defeated** him with the edge of the sword, and took possession of his land from the Arnon to the Jabbok, as far as the people of Ammon; for the border of the people of Ammon *was* fortified.

2. **Nu 32:22-** and the land is **subdued** before the LORD, then afterward you may return and be blameless before the LORD and before Israel; and this land shall be your possession before the LORD.

3. **Nu 32:29-** And Moses said to them: "If the children of Gad and the children of Reuben cross over the Jordan with you, every man armed for battle before the LORD, and the land **is subdued** before you, then you shall give them the land of Gilead as a possession.

4. **Ps 19:13-** Keep back Your servant also from presumptuous *sins;* Let them not **have dominion over** me. Then I shall be blameless, And I shall be innocent of great transgression.

5. **Ps 49:14-** Like sheep they are laid in the grave; Death shall feed on them; The upright **shall have dominion over** them in the morning; And their beauty shall be consumed in the grave, far from their dwelling.

6. **Ps 72:8-** He **shall have dominion** also from sea to sea, And from the River to the ends of the earth.

7. **Ps 110:2-** The LORD shall send the rod of Your strength out of Zion. **Rule** in the midst of Your enemies!

8. **Ps 119:133-** Direct my steps by Your word, And let no iniquity **have dominion over** me.

9. **Dan 11:39-** Thus he shall act against the strongest fortresses with a foreign god, which he shall acknowledge, *and* advance *its* glory; and he shall cause them **to rule over** many, and divide the land for gain.

Κατακυριεύω (2634)

Even in the Old Testament occurrences this word bears the idea of "authority over." Notice Ps 19:13, 49:14, 119:133, Daniel 11:39. Each of these passages carries the idea of dominion or rule "over."

Observations:

Following you will find 1 Peter 5:3 in from several different translations emphasizing the translation of Κατακυριευω.

ASV[53]   neither as **lording it over** the charge allotted to you, but making yourselves ensamples to the flock

DNT[54]   not as **lording it over** your possessions, but being models for the flock.

ISVNT[55] Don't **lord it over** the people entrusted to you, but be examples to the flock.

KJV[56]   Neither as **being lords over** *God's* heritage, but being ensamples to the flock.

NCV[57]   Do not be **like a ruler over** people you are responsible for, but be good examples to them.

NIV[58]   not **lording it over** those entrusted to you, but being examples to the flock.

NKJV[59] nor as **being lords over** those entrusted to you, but being examples to the flock;

NLT[60]   Don't **lord it over** the people assigned to your care, but lead them by your good example.

YLT[61]   neither as **exercising lordship over** the heritages, but patterns becoming of the flock,

---

[53] American Standard Version
[54] Darby's New Translation
[55] International Standard Version (New Testament)
[56] Kin James Version
[57] New Century Version
[58] New International Version
[59] New King James Version
[60] New Living Translation
[61] Young's Literal Translation

Again we see the emphasis on the position of the ruler. He is not to rule "over" the flock. It would seem that New Testament translators accept this idea.

Conclusion:

Κατακυριεύω (2634)

Every occurrence in the New Testament except Rev 17:14 has a negative connotation, as do the majority of references from the Septuagint. This fits well the context of Peter's admonition. Today there are, worldwide, thousands of little "protestant popes." But Peter reminds the elder that he is to lead from among the flock, not as a tyrant but as a shepherd. In 1 Pet 5:3- Peter is telling the elder that he is not to be like the Gentiles or the Pharisees in their leadership styles.

Κλήρων (2634)

The Share

Κλήρων
This "multi-use" word can refer to everything from casting lots to the inheritance promised every saint. One thing is clear from scripture, is that it does not and has never justified some sort of "clergy class" within the church.

New Testament Definitions:

A CONCISE GREEK-ENGLISH DICTIONARY OF THE NEW TESTAMENT
masculine *lot* (of something thrown or drawn to reach a decision); *share, part, place; someone given to another's care* (1 Pe 5:3)

LIDDELL AND SCOTT'S GREEK-ENGLISH LEXICON
a lot; in Homer, each man marks his own lot, and they are thrown into a helmet, and the first which came out was the winning lot.

> **2.** *a casting lots, drawing lots*, Euripides; many officers at Athens obtained their offices *by lot*, as opposed to election (χειροτονία, αἵρεσις), Xenophon, Aristotle; cf. κύαμος II.

> **II.** *an allotment* of land assigned to citizens (cf. κληρουχία), Herodotus, Thucydides, etc.

> **2.** *any piece of land, a portion, farm*, Homer, etc.

> **III.** in Eccl. *the clergy*, as opposed to *the laity*.

NAS HEBREW AND GREEK DICTIONARIES
a lot:—allotted to your charge (1), inheritance (2), lot (1), lots (5), portion (1), share (1).

STRONG'S HEBREW AND GREEK DICTIONARIES
klēros; *klay'-ros;* Probably from G2806 (through the idea of using *bits* of wood, etc., for the purpose); a *die* (for drawing chances); by implication a *portion* (as if so secured); by extension an *acquisition* (especially a *patrimony*, figuratively):—heritage, inheritance, lot, part.

THAYER DEFINITION
   1) an object used in casting or drawing lots, which was either a pebble, or a potsherd, or a bit of wood
   1a) the lots of several persons concerned, inscribed with their names, were thrown together into a vase, which was then shaken, and he whose lot fell out first upon the ground was the one chosen
   2) what is obtained by lot, allotted portion
   2a) a portion of the ministry common to the apostles
   2b) used of the part which one will have in eternal salvation
      2b1) of salvation itself
      2b2) the eternal salvation which God has assigned to the saints
   2c) of persons
      2c1) those whose care and oversight has been assigned to one [allotted charge], used of Christian churches, the administration of which falls to the lot of presbyters

ROBERTSON'S WORD PICTURES OF THE NEW TESTAMENT
The charge allotted to you (*tōn klērōn*). "The charges," "the lots" or "the allotments." See it in Acts 1:17, 25 in this sense. The old word meant a die (Matt 27:25), a portion (Col 1:12; 1 Peter 1:4), here the charges assigned (cf. Acts 17:4). From the adjective *klērikos* come our cleric, clerical, clerk. Wycliff translated it here "neither as having lordship in the clergy."

BARNES' NOTES ON THE NEW TESTAMENT

Over God's heritage—των κλήρων tōn klērōn. Vulgate: "in cleris"—over the clergy. The Greek word here (κλῆρος klēros) is that from which the word "clergy" has been derived; and some have interpreted it here as referring to the clergy, that is, to priests and deacons who are under the authority of a bishop. Such an interpretation, I however, would hardly be adopted now. The word means properly:

   (a) A lot, die, anything used in determining chances;

   (b) A part or portion, such as is assigned by lot; hence,

   (c) An office to which one is designated or appointed, by lot or otherwise; and,

   (d) In general any possession or heritage, Acts 26:18; Col. 1:12.

The meaning here is, "not lording it over the possessions or the heritage of God." The reference is, undoubtedly, to the church, as that which is especially his property; his own in the world. Whitby and others suppose that it refers to the possessions or property of the church; Doddridge explains it—"not assuming dominion over those who fall to your lot," supposing it to mean that they were not to domineer over the particular congregations committed by Providence to their care. But the other interpretation is most in accordance with the usual meaning of the word.

New Testament Occurrences:

Κλήρων (2634)

There are five other occurrences of Κλήρων in the New Testament.

1.   **Luke 23:34-** Then Jesus said, "Father, forgive them, for they do not know what they do." And they divided His garments and cast **lots**.

Note: Here we see the word used as a means of determining something. Similar to rolling dice.

2. **Acts 1:17-** for he was numbered with us and obtained a **part** in this ministry."

   Note: This occurrence is more closely aligned with the idea of its use in 1 Peter. We see it has to do with the portion of the ministerial accountability.

3. **Acts 1:26-** And they cast their **lots**, and the **lot** fell on Matthias. And he was numbered with the eleven apostles.

   Note: As above (Luke 23:34) we see the word used as a means of determining something. Similar to rolling dice.

4. **Acts 8:21-** You have neither part nor **portion** in this matter, for your heart is not right in the sight of God.

   Note: Simon the magician sinned greatly and the Apostles rebuked him. They told him that he had no κληρος in the life given by Christ.

5. **Acts 26:18-** to open their eyes, *in order* to turn *them* from darkness to light, and *from* the power of Satan to God, that they may receive forgiveness of sins and an **inheritance** among those who are sanctified by faith in Me.'

   Note: This use referrs to the inheritance of the saints, a share or portion in eternity.

Κλήρων (2634)

Varied in its use as it is, in 1 Peter it surely refers to the flock and not the elders. Elders are entrusted, by God with those placed in their care.

Observations:

Following you will find 1 Peter 5:3 in from several different translations emphasizing the translation of Κλήρων.

ASV[62] — neither as lording it over the **charge allotted to you**, but making yourselves ensamples to the flock

DNT[63] — not as lording it over **your possessions**, but being models for the flock.

ISVNT[64] — Don't lord it over **the people entrusted to you**, but be examples to the flock.

KJV[65] — Neither as being lords over *God's* **heritage**, but being ensamples to the flock.

NCV[66] — Do not be like a ruler over **people you are responsible for**, but be good examples to them.

NIV[67] — not lording it over **those entrusted to you**, but being examples to the flock.

NKJV[68] — nor as being lords over **those entrusted to you**, but being examples to the flock;

NLT[69] — Don't lord it over **the people assigned to your care**, but lead them by your good example.

YLT[70] — neither as exercising lordship over **the heritages**, but patterns becoming of the flock,

Conclusion:

Notice the emphasis on *responsibility, care* and *trust*. This alone should drive any spiritual leader straight to his knees. God has taken His people, whom He loves enough to allow Jesus to die for them, and entrusts them to us.

---

[62] American Standard Version
[63] Darby's New Translation
[64] International Standard Version (New Testament)
[65] Kin James Version
[66] New Century Version
[67] New International Version
[68] New King James Version
[69] New Living Translation
[70] Young's Literal Translation

Chapter 5

(Textual Criticism)

In 1 Peter Chapter 5:2 we have a textual variance.

The critical text reads:

ἐπισκοποῦντες μὴ ἀναγκαστῶς ἀλλ ἑκουσίως κατὰ θεόν,

overseeing Not by compulsion, but willingly, according to God.

Text Number	Family	Date	Location	Comment
436	Byzantine	XI/XII		
945	Byzantine	XI		
1067	Byzantine	XIV		
1241	Byzantine	XII		
1243	Byzantine	XI		
1409	Byzantine	XIV		
1735	Byzantine	X		

1739	Byzantine	X		
1852	Byzantine	XIII		
2298	Byzantine	XII		
2344^{vid}	Byzantine	XI		
$\mathcal{P}^{72}$	Alexandrian	III/IV	Cologny	Città del Vaticano
$\aleph$	Alexandrian	IV	London	Sinaticus
A	Alexandrian	V	London	Alexandrinus
P	Alexandrian	IX	St. Petersburg	
Ψ	Alexandrian	IX/X	Athos	
81	Alexandrian	1044		
$\aleph^*$	Alexandrian	IV	London	Sinaticus
cop^{sa}	Alexandrian	II		Sahidic
l 596	Western	1146		
it^{ar}	Western	IX	Dublin	Edition: Gwynn
it^{h}	Western	V	Rome	Edition: Jŭlicher/Aland
it^{q}	Western	VI/VII	Munich	Edition: Jŭlicher/Aland
it^{t}	Western	XI	Paris	Edition: Morin
it^{z}	Western	VIII	London	Edition: Buchanan; Thiele; Frede
syr^{h}	Western	616		Harklensis
(syr^{p})	Others	IV		Peshitta
cop^{bo}	Others	II		Bohairic
arm	Others	IV		Kŭnzel; Zohrab
eth,	Others	500		Edition: Hofmann
slav	Others	VIII		Edition: Kalužniacki
Jerome$^{2/3-1/3}$	Others	419/420		
Varimadum^{vid}	Others	445/480		

The Majority reads:

> ἐπισκοποῦντες   μὴ   ἀναγκαστῶς   ἀλλ
> ἑκουσίως,
> overseeing Not by compulsion, but willingly.

Text Number	Family	Date	Location	Comment
K	Byzantine	IX	Moscow	
L	Byzantine	VIII	Rome	
𝔐	Alexandrian			
B	Alexandrian	IV	Vaticanus	Città del Vaticano
l 590	Western	XI	Unknown	
l 884	Western	XIII	Unknown	
l 1441	Western	XIII	Unknown	

Though many thoughtful scholars debate the proper reading of this passage, I am inclined to accept (ἐπισκοποῦντες μὴ ἀναγκαστῶς ἀλλ ἑκουσίως, overseeing Not by compulsion, but willingly).

The internal contradictions of the critical texts along with the sheer numbers of the Majority lead me to the acceptance of this position.

> Shepherd the flock of God, which is among you, serving as overseers, not by compulsion but willingly, not for dishonest gain but eagerly

Chapter 6

(Homiletical Treatment)

1 Peter 5:1-4

The elders who are among you I exhort, I who am a
fellow elder and a witness of the sufferings of Christ, and also
a partaker of the glory that will be revealed: Shepherd the flock
of God which is among you, serving as overseers, not by
compulsion but willingly, not for dishonest gain but eagerly;
nor as being lords over those entrusted to you, but being
examples to the flock; and when the Chief Shepherd appears,
you will receive the crown of glory that does not fade away.

There are many demands placed on those of us in the
ministry. We are asked to be compassionate counselors,
diligent theologians, dynamic speakers and social butterflies. A
pastor needs the tact of a diplomat, the strength of Samson, the
patience of Job, the wisdom of Solomon--and a cast-iron

stomach. The following is an actual add placed in the *Milwaukee Sentinel*:

> Wanted- A rector for St. James' Church. He must possess all Christian graces and a few worldly ones; must have such tact and disposition as will enable him to side with all parties in the parish an all points, giving offense to none; should possess a will of his own, but agree with all the vestry; must be socially inclined and of dignified manners--affable to all, neither running after the wealthy nor turning his back upon the poor; a man of high-low church tendencies preferred. Must be willing to preach first-class sermons and do first-class work on second-class compensation--salary should not be so much of an object as the desire to be a zealous laborer in the vineyard; should be able to convince all that they are miserable sinners without giving offense. Each sermon must be short, but complete in itself--full of old-fashioned theology in modern dress: deep but polished, and free from the eloquence peculiar to newly-graduated theologians; should be young enough to be enthusiastic, but possess judgment of one of ripe years and experience. Only he who possesses the above qualifications need apply. To such a one will be given steady employment for a term of years.

When trying to determine our job descriptions we would be amiss if we neglected the great words of Peter in 1 Peter 5: 1-4.

PETER'S PREFACE

Peter was a Fellow-Elder

Peter begins by building a common bond, *"The elders who are among you I exhort, I who am a fellow elder..."*

Peter could have identified himself in a number of ways. He could have said "Peter, so named by Christ Himself, the Apostle who first recognized Jesus as the Messiah, and chief among the believers ..." But he did not. He simply and humbly called himself a "fellow-elder." Peter was a man who had led the flock. He was in fact commissioned to do so by Christ Himself.

In John 21: 14-17 we find Jesus speaking to Peter after the resurrection,

> This *is* now the third time Jesus showed Himself to His disciples after He was raised from the dead. So when they had eaten breakfast, Jesus said to Simon Peter, "Simon, *son* of Jonah, do you love Me more than these?"
>
> He said to Him, "Yes, Lord; You know that I love You."
>
> He said to him, "Feed My lambs."
>
> He said to him again a second time, "Simon, *son* of Jonah, do you love Me?"
>
> He said to Him, "Yes, Lord; You know that I love You."
>
> He said to him, "Tend My sheep."
>
> He said to him the third time, "Simon, *son* of Jonah, do you love Me?" Peter was grieved because He said to him the third time, "Do you love Me?"

And he said to Him, "Lord, You know all things; You know that I love You."

Jesus said to him, "Feed My sheep."

Notice the terminology that Jesus used here. "Feed My lambs." "Tend My sheep." "Feed My sheep." Peter was a fisherman not a shepherd, yet Christ chose to use the vocabulary of the shepherd when speaking of His people.

Peter was commissioned by Christ on the banks of that muddy river that day and he strove to fulfill that commission. So, peter, with humility and respect opens this section of scripture identifying himself with the elders.

He also identifies himself in two other ways:

Peter was a Witness
and a witness of the sufferings of Christ, and also a partaker of the glory that will be revealed:

Was Peter a witness of the sufferings of Christ? Remember in the garden, when the temple guards, led by Judas, came to arrest Jesus? It was Peter who drew his sword and attacked a servant. Jesus commanded him to lower his sword, then surrendered Himself to them. We read that the other disciples scattered, but not Peter. He followed, at a distance, the Lord and even went into the courtyard with the Christ and His captors.

It was most likely in that courtyard that Jesus was beaten by the guards, spit upon and even had a crown made of thorns pressed into His brow. Peter most certainly witnessed the sufferings of Christ.

Peter was an Inheritor

and also a partaker of the glory that will be revealed:

It is interesting to note that earlier in this letter Peter spoke of "an inheritance incorruptible and undefiled and that does not fade away, reserved in heaven for you." This description of the Saint's reward is revisited twice in our text. First here in Peter's description of himself as a partaker of the glory to come, and at the end as we will see later.

Peter is again identifying with his readers. As Christians we are all promised this inheritance, and Peter was using this to again, build a commonality with the elders that he was addressing.

PETER'S PRINCIPLES

"The elders who are among you I exhort, I who am a fellow elder..." Peter is writing this with a purpose, he is exhorting, or teaching those elders who would read this epistle. Remember what Paul said to Timothy in 2 Timothy 3:16-17,

All Scripture *is* given by inspiration of God, and *is* profitable for doctrine, for reproof, for correction, for instruction in righteousness, that the man of God may be complete, thoroughly equipped for every good work.

Peter is not simply writing this for something to do. He has some divine instructions that he has to delineate, equipping the elders to "every good work."

The Mission

"Shepherd the flock of God which is among you, serving as overseers…"

First is the command to *"Shepherd the flock of God which is among you."* The Greek verb here is in what is called the "imperative mood." That means that it is imperative, or crucial for our ministry. It is not a suggestion, but a command.

"Shepherd the flock of God which is among you." Please notice something here. Where is the flock? Peter did not write, "Shepherd the flock of God that is subordinate to you," or "that is beneath you" He assumed that the elder was among the flock, in their lives, part of their community. There is an old Russian Proverb that says, "Without a shepherd, sheep are not a flock."

The idea of shepherding comes from one of that region's chief occupations. It is interesting to note that you cannot drive sheep, you cannot stand above them and command them one way or another, a shepherd has to get down with them and lead them.

The Method

"Shepherd the flock of God which is among you, serving as overseers,"

"Serving as overseers" Do not misunderstand; there is a certain amount of authority that is placed on the shoulders of an elder. In fact the Bible is clear that with reward, there is also responsibility and accountability placed on the elder. But

notice the emphasis of this whole passage. Peter emphasizes the shepherd role far above the role as overseer.

So how are we to serve as overseers, while being a shepherd?

Willingly

"Serving as overseers, not by compulsion but willingly..."

First we are to serve willingly. We are to submit our selves to the will of God with little or no regard for ourselves. We must be willing subjects before we can be God's chosen leaders.

We cannot serve out of some since of obligation. How many of us in our Christianity have been pressured into leading some Sunday-school class that we had no business trying to teach. Do it willingly. God doesn't want you to take an office in the church in this pouting spirit: "Well, if you can't get anybody else to do it, I'll do it."

Freely

"Serving as overseers... not for dishonest gain but eagerly..." There is a website where one can go and book a "Christian Speaker" for an event. Now how do you think that the hundreds of speakers are organized? By denomination? No. By doctrine? No. Oh, I know by geographic location... right? No. You log into this website and you search for a "Christian speaker" based on what you are willing to pay. Prices begin at two thousand dollars per appearance and they go right on up from there.

Again, do not misunderstand; Scripture is clear that ministers are to be cared for financially, but that must NEVER be the motive.

There is a story about a church that was trying to start a building fund. Now, in the same town there was this rotten old man who cared for nothing but his money. He had foreclosed on the retirement home, evicted the orphanage and sold the cemetery to a strip mall. Well, when this old miser died, his brother approached the pastor of this little church.

"Hey Preacher, I understand that you are trying to build onto your little church here."

"That's right," said the pastor.

"Well you preach my brother's funeral tomorrow and you say that he was a saint, and I'll give you two hundred thousand dollars toward your little project."

The next day the preacher approached the pulpit to address all who were in attendance at the funeral. The whole town had heard about the offer and waited with baited breath. The deceased's brother sat on the front row looking triumphant and the pastor spoke.

"This man who we are here to lay to rest, was a mean, rotten, cheat. He was a philanderer, and a wretch. But, compared to his brother he was a saint."

Humbly

"Serving as overseers... nor as being lords over those entrusted to you, but being examples to the flock..."

Today there are, worldwide, thousands of little "protestant popes." But Peter reminds the elder that he is to lead from among the flock, not as a tyrant but as a shepherd.

There are tree main principals that we as leaders can derive from this one little section:

1. **Not being Lords**- There is only one Lord. There is
   only one mediator. There is only one Great
   Shepherd. And, I can personally guarantee that none
   of us are Him. The theme is consistent throughout
   this passage. It is clear and reasonable, "servant-
   leadership."

   The Greek word used here is a compound word that
   means to rule over. Peter uses this very powerful
   word deliberately. It speaks of tyranny, and
   oppression. There are churches that are like that.
   The pastor is the king of his own little domain. The
   problem is that the domain is neither little nor his.

2. **Those entrusted to you**- Elders are entrusted, by
   God with those placed in their care. There is an
   emphasis on *responsibility, care* and *trust*. This
   alone should drive any spiritual leader straight to his
   knees. God has taken His people, whom He loves
   enough to allow Jesus to die for them, and entrusts
   them to us.

   The writer of Hebrews said to believers, *"Obey
   those who rule over you, and be submissive, for they
   watch out for your souls, as those who must give
   account. Let them do so with joy and not with grief,
   for that would be unprofitable for you."* -Hebrews
   13:17

   The biblical author understood the responsibility
   placed on the elder by God, *"as those who must give
   account..."* God has entrusted His flock to the
   leadership of the local church but they are not
   without responsibility.

3. **Being examples-** Now is when we get to the meat of the method. In telling us how to be elders, thus far, Peter has mostly dealt with the "do nots." But now we have the "do."

Discipleship. Mentorship. Modeling. These are all methods of learning, and this is precisely what Peter is talking about. Again, let us hear from the author of Hebrews, *"Remember those who rule over you, who have spoken the word of God to you, whose faith follow, considering the outcome of their conduct."*

–Hebrews 13:7

Look at the two phrases, *"whose faith follow"* and *"considering the outcome of their conduct."* The writer is telling the saints the same thing that Peter is telling the elders. Peter says to the elders, "be examples to the flock." The author of Hebrews says to the flock, "use your elders as examples." Dr. J Vernon McGee addressed this passage and said, "In other words, an elder should exercise his ministry in the right manner, not driving but leading, not domineering but setting an example. It is a work, therefore, in which he ought to be an example to the flock. I do not think that a preacher should get into the pulpit and browbeat his congregation to do something that he actually is not doing himself. I made it a practice never to ask my congregation to give to any cause to which I didn't also give. I do not think we have a right to make a demand of other folk that we are not doing ourselves."[71]

---

[71]McGee, J. Vernon, *Thru the Bible with J. Vernon McGee*, Nashville: Thomas Nelson Publishers 2000

PETER'S PLEDGE

"and when the Chief Shepherd appears, you will receive the crown of glory that does not fade away."

Look at the assurance that Peter exudes as he writes these words. One afternoon, Peter and several others were in a field with the resurrected Christ, when without warning He ascended out of sight. Not knowing what to do next they just stood there, staring up into the clouds that had obscured Him from their vision. As they stood there, we know not how long, they were visited by two if God's angels who said, *"Men of Galilee, why do you stand gazing up into heaven? This same Jesus, who was taken up from you into heaven, will so come in like manner as you saw Him go into heaven."* –Acts 1:11

Peter, no doubt, never forgot that day nor that promise. And so he comforts us with the words of comfort that he had received so very long ago, *"and when the Chief Shepherd appears..."*

Notice also, Peter's description of Christ, "Chief Shepherd." All through this passage Peter has reminded us that we are to be shepherds, and now he is connecting that ministry with Christ Himself. Do we truly see Christ as the Chief Shepherd? How do we understand the concept of a divine shepherd?

A.W. Tozer said, "The gradual disappearance of the idea and feeling of majesty from the Church is a sign and a portent. Our God has now become our servant to wait on our will. "The Lord is my **shepherd**," we say, instead of "The

Lord is my shepherd," and the difference is as wide as the world[72]."

"and when the Chief Shepherd appears, you will receive the crown of glory that does not fade away." At His coming the elders are promised a reward. See, Peter said that we are not to seek glory, power, or wealth as ministers here on earth. But, when Jesus, the Chief Shepherd returns, we will receive all of that.

Glory, as we hear Jesus' words of encouragement as He places this eternal crown on our heads.

Power, as we stand in the presence of the resurrected Lord as His servants, having done the work of the ministry.

Wealth, as we inherit all of the richness of heaven and dwell in His presence for eternity.

The words are powerful and the challenge is clear. We are called into a hazardous duty, yet commanded to enter in, not with military pride and bearing, but with humility as a servant. May we commit to pray for one another that this sure calling is indicative of our own ministries. That when the Lord calls us home, we are remembered as examples and not tyrants.

---

[72] A.W. Tozer, Born After Midnight. Christianity Today, Vol. 41, no. 5.

Selected Bibliography

Aland, Kurt. *The Greek New Testament with Dictionary*.
    Edmonds: United Bible Society 1966

Bullinger, E. W. *Figures of Speech Used in the Bible*. Grand
    Rapids: Baker 1968

Comfort, Philip Wesley - Ed. *The Origin of the Bible*.
    Wheaton: Tyndale

Dana, H. E. and Julius R. Mantey. *A Manual Grammar of the
    Greek New Testament*. Upper Saddle River: Prentice
    Hall 1927

Farstad, Arthur. *The NKJV Greek English Interlinear New
    Testament*. Nashville: Nelson 1994

Grassmick, John D. *Principles and Practice of Greek Exegesis*
    Dallas: Dallas Theological Seminary 1974

Hastings, James - Ed. *Hastings' Dictionary of the Bible*. New
    York: Hendrickson 1909

Hatch, Edwin and Hery A. Redpath. *Concordance to the Septuagint.* Grand Rapids: Baker 1897

Hodges, C. Zane. *The Greek New Testament according to the Majority Text.* Nashville: Nelson 1985

Kubo, Sakae. *A Reader's Greek-English Lexicon of the New Testament.* Zondervan

Lightfoot, J. B. *Biblical Essays.* Hendrickson 1893

Perschbacher, Wesley J. *The New Analytical Greek Lexicon.* Peabody: Hendrickson 1990

Ramm, Bernard. *Protestant Biblical Interpretation.* Grand Rapids: Baker 1970

Robertson, Archibald. *Word Pictures in the New Testament Set 1 – 6.* Broadman

Strong, James. *The New Strong's Exhaustive Concordance of the Bible.* Nashville: Nelson 1964

Summers, Ray. *Essentials of New Testament Greek.* Nashville: Broadman & Holman 1995

Vine, W. E. *Vine's Complete Expository Dictionary of Old & New Testament Words.* Nashville: Nelson 1984

Wallace, Daniel B. *Greek Grammar Beyond the Basics.* Grand Rapids: Zondervan 1996

Wallace, Daniel B. *The Basics of New Testament Syntax.* Grand Rapids: Zondervan 2000

Walvoord, John F. and Roy B. Zuck. *The Bible Knowledge*

Wiersbe, Warren W. *The Bible Exposition Commentary.* Colorado Springs: Victor 1989

Wiersbe, Warren W. *Wiersbe's Expository Outlines on the New Testament.* Colorado Springs:

Wigram, George V. and Ralph D. Winter. *The Word Study New Testament and Concordance.* Wheaton: Wheaton 1972

Zodhiates, Spiros. *The Complete Word Study Dictionary of the New Testament.* Chattanooga: AMG Publishers 1992

www.ingramcontent.com/pod-product-compliance
Lightning Source LLC
Chambersburg PA
CBHW071949100426
42736CB00042B/2614